Diagnosing Your Team

A Practical Guide for Understanding and Transforming Teams

By

Grant Thompson, Psy.D.

Copyright © by Grant Thompson

Author photo by Lindsey Wilde

ISBN 978-1-64970-954-7

For additional copies of this book go to
www.thompsonconsulting.com

Printed in Korea

Dedication

For my children: Audrey, Owen, and Hope

Acknowledgments

Special thanks to my terrific work team (Natalie Hilde, Karleigh Deeds, Lindsey Wilde and Tom Kelley).

Table of Contents

Section I: Diagnosing Your Team 1

Introduction 3

Chapter 1: Defining Team Health 7

Chapter 2: Diagnosing Team Leadership 13

Chapter 3: Diagnosing Team Communication 18

Chapter 4: Diagnosing Team Trust 23

Chapter 5: Diagnosing Team Culture 28

Chapter 6: Diagnosing Team Performance 33

Chapter 7: Top Ten Symptoms of a Sick Team 38

Section II: Assessing Team Health 45

Chapter 8: The Diagnosis: The Assessment of
          Team Health 47

    - Overview of scoring and subtests
    - Participating in the ATH (30 items)
    - Analyzing your team's overall score
    - Analyzing the subtests
    - What do your scores really mean?

Section III: Case Studies 57

Chapter 9:   Case Study #1: The "Feel Good" Team 59

Chapter 10: Case Study #2: The "Passive-Aggressive" Team 65

Chapter 11: Case Study #3: The "Frozen in Time" Team 71

Section IV: Transforming Your Team............................ 79

Chapter 12: Do Activities and Exercises Build Teams?........81

Chapter 13: Turning Around a Troubled Team 86

Chapter 14: Transitioning from Average to Elite................92

Conclusion 97

Section I

Diagnosing Your Team

Introduction

"In the long history of humankind, those who learned to collaborate most effectively have prevailed."
– Charles Darwin

Traci McGregor found herself in the middle of the COVID-19 storm. The media had just reported that the first COVID patients had been diagnosed in Boise, Idaho, when suddenly there was chaos at the St. Luke's Medical Center Emergency Department where McGregor is Director of Nursing. "It had actually been a quiet day when all of a sudden the ED completely blew up," said McGregor. "There were patients everywhere. They were in the lobby. They were out front. They were all wanting to be tested to see if they had the virus."

From the moment the crisis started, McGregor relied heavily on her four-nurse leadership team, who were responsible for more than 100 ED staff. "There's nothing quite like a crisis to tell you about the strength of your leadership team," said McGregor. "During a crisis, people either respond or they pretty much disappear. My team really responded."

McGregor's leadership team was responsible for the testing of thousands of patients while also facing the constant risk of

Introduction

exposure to the virus. According to McGregor, the nurse leaders also had to be "part medical professional and part psychologist" as they helped support dozens of tired, anxious and stressed-out staff members. Frankly, many teams would crack under these kinds of pressures, but McGregor's shined. "I knew they were a talented team, but they exceeded my expectations," she said. "They just kept stepping up to each challenge."

The story of McGregor's nurse leadership team is inspiring. Unfortunately, it's also uncommon. **The reality is that most teams are unsuccessful. Multiple studies have found that more than 60 percent of work teams are unproductive and fail to achieve their assigned goals** (Parisi-Carew 2009). Another 30 percent typically perform at an average level and achieve marginal results. This leaves a whopping 10 percent of American work teams performing at a truly elite level.

In spite of these discouraging statistics, corporate America continues to be dominated by work teams. Ninety-eight percent of American employees are part of at least one team. Large corporations often have thousands of teams gathering on a weekly basis. Sales teams, project teams, virtual teams, self-directed teams, troubleshooting teams, interworking teams, and cross-functional teams are just a handful of the groups you'll find gathering consistently. Candidly, I'm clueless as to the purpose of many of these teams.

Don't get me wrong. McGregor and her colleagues demonstrated that there's nothing quite as inspiring and energizing as being part of a truly cohesive, high-performing team. In my own career, I've been fortunate to be part of a consulting team that is talented, supportive, and highly productive. However, take it from someone

"There's nothing quite like a crisis to tell you about the strength of your leadership team."

— Traci McGregor, Emergency Department Director of Nursing, St. Luke's Hospital

Introduction

who has assessed and coached hundreds of different teams over the past 25 years, truly elite teams are the exception, not the norm.

So, what ails America's work teams? Why are so few teams healthy and productive while most teams are barely stable or even critically ill? In this book, I examine in detail the reasons for the poor health of so many work teams. I also explore the traits common to the rare exceptional teams.

The book includes a variety of stories about teams I've worked with over the years. Some of the stories are insightful and inspirational while others are humorous and, frankly, hard to believe. In addition, the book includes interviews with some of the best team leaders I've had the opportunity to observe. These leaders share their secrets to success as well as their greatest team challenges and failures. All the team scenarios presented in the book actually occurred. However, in some instances, identifying information (names, job titles, companies, etc.) has been changed to respect confidentiality.

The book begins by examining the five different components that are crucial to team health. It explores the 10 most common reasons teams fail and also examines the characteristics common in truly elite teams. Finally, the book provides you with an opportunity to examine the health of your own team. In Chapter 8 of the book, readers can participate in a brief survey called the Assessment of Team Health (ATH). This tool provides a snapshot of your current level of team functioning, as well as suggestions for boosting team performance. So, let's get started. It's time to begin transforming your team.

CHAPTER 1

Defining Team Health

"If everyone is moving forward together then success takes care of itself." – Henry Ford

The most dysfunctional executive team I ever worked with looked terrific on paper. The group consisted mostly of Stanford and Ivy League graduates, many of whom possessed advanced degrees. All of the executives held at least a vice president title and some of them had even fancier titles like Chief Strategy Officer and Executive Vice President of Human Capital. The group made a tremendous first impression, greeting guests with firm handshakes and pleasant smiles. They were articulate, well-dressed, polite, and a good-looking crew. On the surface, they appeared to be the perfect leadership team.

The CEO of the company had asked me to come and observe some of the team's interactions because they were having some "communication and morale challenges." Frankly, about halfway through that first meeting, I was wondering if he might be mistaken. They listened intently to one another, often nodding approval or smiling. There wasn't a great deal of discussion or debate. However, frankly, they didn't seem to disagree on much.

It wasn't until the meeting adjourned that things started to get interesting. The nine participants politely excused themselves, divided up, and regrouped in separate offices. It was then that the knives came out. What followed was a behind-the-scenes, passive-aggressive, no-holds-barred assault on their Executive Team colleagues. One member railed that the Vice President of Finance had a "giant-sized ego" rivaled only by his "enormous mouth." Another member complained that the Vice President of Human Resources was "a snake in the grass looking for employees to devour." A third member of this inspiring leadership team complained that the CEO's "next original idea would be his first."

Sound ridiculous? Seem like something you might hear in a junior high lunchroom? Unfortunately, these hostile, cutthroat practices are not all that uncommon in corporate America. Highly educated, extremely intelligent executives attempting to utilize their high IQs to achieve personal agendas instead of doing what is in the best interest of their teams.

Essential Components of Healthy Teams

Whenever examining the health of a team, I begin by evaluating five essential components. They include 1) leadership, 2) communication, 3) trust, 4) culture, and 5) performance. Unfortunately, the team I described above was critically ill in all five areas. Before we continue to examine additional teams, let's take a closer look at the five components:

Leadership

Healthy teams almost always have strong leadership. In fact, in more than 25 years working with hundreds of different teams, I've yet to find a truly exceptional team being managed

"Healthy teams communicate proactively, sharing information before being asked."

by a poor leader. Characteristics of strong team leaders include the ability to 1) define the purpose and goals of the team; 2) build commitment and confidence; 3) model effective communication and resolve conflicts; 4) provide development opportunities; 5) demonstrate humility by "getting in the trenches," when necessary; and 6) focus intensely on results.

Communication

Healthy teams have open lines of communication. Team members communicate assertively (remaining direct and respectful) with one another and aren't afraid to disagree and debate in order to reach good decisions. Rather than one or two people dominating team discussions, all members provide input. Healthy teams communicate proactively, sharing information before being asked. Team members actively listen to one another and use positive nonverbal communication to encourage the exchange of ideas and information.

Trust

Healthy teams operate in an environment where members trust and look out for one another. Individual members are willing to take risks without fearing repercussions. Most importantly, team members are willing to reveal mistakes and ask questions when they are confused. This is important because the earlier mistakes are identified and questions are answered, the sooner challenges can be addressed. When team members trust one another, they are more comfortable disagreeing and challenging one another's ideas, which ultimately results in better decisions.

Culture

Healthy teams have a positive, high-energy culture. Specific characteristics common in teams with positive culture include low

Chapter 1 Defining Team Health

turnover, openness to change, opportunities for development, and a common understanding of team goals. One of the telltale signs that a team has a strong culture is that people want to join. It isn't because team members receive more money or benefits; it's that they want to be part of the positive environment.

Performance

Healthy teams achieve results. You can think your teammates are the greatest people in the world. However, if you aren't getting results, your team isn't successful. High-functioning teams set high standards for performance that are clearly defined, measurable, and are consistently met by individual members and the team as a whole. Healthy teams utilize metrics allowing members to evaluate their performance and the connection between the work of the team and the overall success of the organization.

Essential Components of Healthy Teams

Chapter 1 Defining Team Health

Every team is a little different because it is composed of unique individuals with varying personalities, backgrounds, and skill sets. However, what truly high-productive, high-functioning teams have in common is that they are all strong when it comes to the above five characteristics. Most teams have strengths, but few possess all five essential components of healthy teams.

CHAPTER 2

Diagnosing Team Leadership

"Leaders should strive for authenticity over perfection."
– Sheryl Sandberg, COO of Facebook

The CEO of a 200-employee software organization strides to the front of the room to deliver the "State of the Company" address. He readies his notes, clicks his first PowerPoint slide, and proceeds to bury his audience in an avalanche of clichés related to teams and teamwork. He opens by pointing out that "great synergy" has developed in the past year between sales and operations. He then informs the group that the company is "only as strong as its weakest link." He shifts gears and points out that "there's no 'I' in team." Then, finally, the humble leader finishes with one of the classics: "It's about we, not me."

By the time the executive is finished with his cliché-filled diatribe, about half the audience is snickering and the rest are half asleep. The lesson here is pretty simple. Inspirational speeches filled with platitudes don't make someone a great team leader. Now don't get me wrong. Making some very specific, positive comments about work teams in front of the rest of the company is terrific for employee morale. However, what's most important is how managers communicate and lead their employees day to day. In other words, a once a year speech will not compensate for poor leadership the other 364 days.

Unfortunately, the numbers are ugly when it comes to how average employees feel about their leaders. In her 2017 article, *Ten Signs of Poor Leadership*, Silvia Pencak points out some frightening statistics, including the fact that three out of four employees report that their boss is the worst part of their jobs. In addition, two-thirds of employees say they would take a new boss over a pay raise.

The most common complaint employees have about their bosses is that they have poor communication skills. In a study of more than 1,000 American employees, a shocking 90 percent said their managers needed to improve their communication skills (Solomon 2016). Some other less than inspiring statistics about bosses include:

- Sixty-three percent failed to recognize employee achievements
- Fifty-seven percent did not provide clear directions
- Thirty-nine percent offered no constructive criticism
- Thirty-six percent did not know their employees' names

Nancy Lebold, Vice President of Merchandising for Food 4 Less, understands why so few employees are happy with their bosses. "A lot of leaders in the corporate world are phonies," she said. "They're simply trying to say what they need to say to get results. Early in my career, all I cared about was getting results. It took me a few years to realize how much I had to learn."

"Inspirational speeches filled with platitudes don't make someone a great team leader."

Chapter 2 Diagnosing Team Leadership

For Lebold, the light bulb went on early in her career when she went through a 360-degree leadership survey, an assessment from all directions—peers, supervisors, and direct reports. "The first survey ever conducted on me was brutal," she said. "It basically painted me as some kind of cold-hearted machine. Employees didn't want to work for me and they certainly weren't performing anywhere near their peak. I cried after I received those results and then I committed to being a better leader."

Meeting Lebold today it is hard to envision the "heartless," authoritarian leader she described. She smiles like a proud parent when answering questions about members of her team and embraces the uniqueness of her different employees. "Early in my career, I wanted them all to act like me. Now, that's the last thing I want," she joked. "I've learned each employee is motivated a little differently and it's my job to understand them. At this point, I'm more of a facilitator than a leader."

One of the keys to Lebold's turnaround was consciously focusing more on "the soft skills." She focuses on doing a better job of "listening" and "asking for input." These are among some of the key behaviors outlined by author and leadership expert John Whitney, who has extensively examined eight different factors that contribute to effective leadership including:

1. **People skills**: The leader is easy to communicate with, has an open-door policy, and gives praise and critique accordingly.

2. **Honesty**: The leader says what he or she will do and then does it.
3. **Decisiveness**: The leader gathers data before making a decision, but for the most part, decisions will be final when made.
4. **Result-driven**: The leader identifies goals and holds employees accountable for achieving them.
5. **Delegates and motivates**: The leader assigns tasks with benefits and consequences outlined.
6. **Accepts responsibility**: The leader does not blame others—ever.
7. **Team player**: The leader is open to input and collaborates with coworkers including those in other business units.
8. **Innovative**: The leader knows that just because it was done one way in the past does not mean it must be done identically now.

Lebold has participated in multiple 360 surveys since receiving her "brutal results" nearly two decades ago. These days the data tend to be glowing, but she learns something each time. "I've learned that you have to be genuine. Leadership is more than just giving a good speech or spouting a bunch of leadership clichés. It's something you have to constantly work at."

CHAPTER 3

Diagnosing Team Communication

"You can have brilliant ideas, but if you can't get them across, your ideas won't get you anywhere."
– Lee Iacocca, Former CEO of Chrysler

Email has revolutionized business. It ranks right up there with copy machines and mobile phones among the greatest business innovations of all time. However, email, as well as other forms of electronic communication, also causes more chaos, confusion, and hurt feelings than anything else in the workplace.

In fact, email has become the weapon of choice among dysfunctional communicators. From the safety of your own office, you can send a snarky, critical email message to a coworker while simultaneously copying that individual's boss. For that matter, you can copy half the employees in the company to ensure maximum humiliation. Direct, respectful communication? Who needs it when you can blast people on email and never have to face them? As Ryan Holmes, the CEO of Hootsuite said, "Email is familiar. It's comfortable. It's easy to use. But it might just be the biggest killer of time and productivity in the office today."

Chapter 3 Diagnosing Team Communication

Allowing employees to run wild with electronic communication is one way to ensure your team will suffer from poor morale. It is essential that organizations have policies to discourage these electronic "hit jobs" and managers be willing to hold employees accountable when they communicate inappropriately. In addition to proper use of electronic communication, below are some additional suggestions for ensuring strong team communication.

Model Effective Communication

If the leader of a team doesn't model effective communication, there is little to no chance that the members of the team will communicate appropriately. The leader of the team I described above was a very nice guy, but a passive individual, who rarely modeled assertive communication. One of the reasons the team's communication became so dysfunctional is that he refused to confront members who engaged in destructive, behind-the-scenes communication.

Stop Being so Secretive

Employees become paranoid and start gossiping when they feel company leaders and coworkers are being secretive. The more transparent organizations are with information, the less employees wrongly fill in the blanks. Joel Gasgoigne, CEO of the social media company Buffer, believes in total transparency when it comes to information, including financials, strategy, executive salaries, etc. "Transparency breeds trust and trust is the foundation of great teamwork," said Gascoigne.

Ask Open-Ended Questions

If you ask "yes or no" questions during team meetings, you'll get "yes and no" answers. Asking open-ended questions

> *Transparency breeds trust and trust is the foundation of great teamwork.*

— Joel Gascoigne, CEO of Buffer

encourages discussion and debate and leads to more creative problem solving. In addition, if topics are discussed and/or debated during the meeting, they are less likely to be the subject of gossip later on.

Eliminate Business Jargon

Business jargon is another obstacle to successful communication. Leaders who utilize jargon and business clichés often confuse coworkers and they can also be seen as arrogant or "full of themselves." Encourage leaders in your organization to use plain language to facilitate better organizational communication.

Stay Focused

If you have more than two or three high-level team goals, you have too many. At all times, employees need to know the primary focus of the team. Jim Collins, the author of the bestseller *Good to Great*, believes team leaders are asking for trouble if participants are focusing on multiple goals. "If you have more than three priorities, you don't have any," said Collins.

You can count Teresa Mitzel, Head of Biological Operations at Syngenta Seeds, as someone who believes that clear, effective communication is the "most important factor in team success." Mitzel, a 27-year veteran of Syngenta, is highly intelligent and possesses a Master's Degree in Genetics. However, her explanation of effective communication is incredibly simple. "I'm constantly asking the same two questions of my employees and peers," she said. "I ask 'How are you?' and 'How can I help you?'"

Syngenta is a global agriculture company and Mitzel manages employees all over the world, many of whom speak English as a second language. These communication challenges make her focus on communication fundamentals all the more important. "Understanding one another is the biggest challenge in any company, but especially in an international company like Syngenta," said Mitzel.

Mitzel employs some very concrete strategies to make certain team communication effective. "I often finish conversations with my coworkers by saying things like, 'let me summarize this so I can make certain we're on the same page.' I'll also say things like 'let me rephrase that in case I wasn't clear.'"

Mitzel said the highest functioning team she had ever served on in her career was the North American Vegetable Leadership Team at Syngenta. In her opinion, the success was "all about communication." "We were able to say what was on our minds without being judged. We didn't use lots of business language. When we had disagreements, we would passionately make our case, but we weren't disrespectful."

According to Mitzel, the communication translated to performance. The North American Vegetable Team achieved some of the best numbers in the company, including double-digit revenue growth. "We were direct with one another. We were respectful. We didn't use a bunch of lingo, and we certainly didn't take shots at one another using email."

CHAPTER 4

Diagnosing Team Trust

"Trust is the glue of life. It's the most essential ingredient in effective communication."
– Stephen Covey

Mary Chronin led her first team in the St. Luke's Health System at the age of 24. Many of her employees were more than twice her age. Chronin was extremely green, but bright, eager, and, perhaps most importantly, humble enough to know that she didn't have everything figured out. "I spent a lot of time asking questions in that first leadership role," said Chronin. "Obviously, most of my employees had more industry knowledge than I did."

More than 15 years later, Associate Vice President of Operations at St. Luke's, Chronin has developed a reputation for improving struggling teams. In total, she has led more than a dozen different teams and/or departments, including Nurse Staffing, Accreditation, Lab, Patient Experience, Emergency Management, Patient Access, Employee Safety, Transfer Center, Provider Outreach, Facilities, Language Services, and Real Estate.

Chapter 4 Diagnosing Team Trust

One characteristic Chronin often finds in struggling teams is a lack of trust. "Sometimes the employees don't trust leadership and sometimes they don't trust one another," said Chronin. "As a result, communication on the team is poor and often destructive."

A few years ago, Google set out to determine the most important characteristic of a successful team. They conducted extensive research and even code-named the study "Project Aristotle." At the end of the day, **Google determined that "psychological safety," or trust, was the single most important team attribute.** The study found that "an individual's perception of taking a risk, and the response his or her teammates will have to taking that risk was most crucial."

In addition, Google concluded that, "In a team with high psychological safety, teammates feel safe to take risks around their team members. They feel confident that no one on the team will embarrass or punish anyone else for admitting a mistake, asking a question, or offering a new idea."

So given Google's conclusions, what's the key to turning around a team that lacks trust? "I think the first thing you have to do is call out the unhealthy behaviors," said Chronin. "I often find that team members are acting like victims and you have to stop the victim cycle and focus the team on what they can control," said Chronin.

Chronin is an upbeat, high-energy leader who presents herself with a big smile. However, her positive demeanor should not be confused with being a pushover when it comes to tackling team dysfunction. "It's pretty simple. We discuss the goals and

"Avoidance never works. We've got to put issues on the table and deal with them."

— Mary Chronin, Associate Vice President, St. Luke's Health System.

vision of the team and I ask them to get on board. If they can't, they need to evaluate their options. There is no option to continue to spin and be disruptive. The only option is to either contribute to the team's success or leave the team. It is important to be clear about that."

According to research conducted by the Center for Creative Leadership (Reina & Reina 2017), teams have better attendance and higher performance in trusting environments. Employees are also more likely to share information freely and attempt innovative strategies when part of a trusting team, because they know coworkers will support them if they make mistakes.

Building trust starts with a team leader who is humble and willing to take responsibility when things go wrong. If your leader starts pointing fingers during tough times, your team has no chance of developing trust. The team leader also needs to model open communication and demonstrate a willingness to consider alternative opinions. Micromanaging is perhaps the most obvious sign that a team leader lacks trust in his or her employees. It doesn't exactly show faith in an employee when their supervisor is looking over their shoulder all day.

When it comes to a lack of trust among team members, there are a variety of symptoms, including:

1. Increased gossip
2. More office cliques
3. Lack of engagement
4. Fear of acknowledging mistakes
5. Lack of participation in meetings
6. Avoidance of conflict

"Avoidance never works," said Chronin. "We've got to put issues on the table and deal with them. And folks that aren't willing to do that need to move on. There is no third choice. Stay on the team and be a teammate or get off the bus. … There is nothing more destructive than allowing bad behavior within the team."

CHAPTER 5

Diagnosing Team Culture

"Culture eats strategy for breakfast" – Peter Drucker

Billy Salts is the definition of the American dream. In 2012, Salts, an electrician, started his own business with one employee and a $20,000 loan. In 7 years, he has built Magic Valley Electric into a multimillion-dollar business that employs more than one hundred people. Salts has no college education. In fact, he dropped out of Utah State on the second day of orientation because he determined, "School wasn't really for me." However, Salts has defied the odds and thrived in the business world. So what's his secret? Why has he succeeded while so many better educated business owners have failed? Perhaps it's because Salts is on a never-ending quest to create the perfect company culture.

"When we have a Management Team meeting, we spend about 70 percent of our time focusing on culture and 30 percent on operations and the financials," said Salts. "We really don't talk much about profit margins and cost cutting in our meetings. We're much more likely to talk about things like leadership or morale."

Salts, who greets employees and clients with a big smile and an energy level bordering on mania, has pretty much blown up all the traditional corporate norms when it comes to building culture. For instance, he completely rejects the idea that company leaders should avoid socializing with employees. In fact, he believes that's the very best way to build culture. "We do bike rides, picnics, softball games, parades and fireworks with our employees," said Salts. "We work together and socialize together. We want to have great relationships with our employees and their families. We feel like that translates into a great culture."

Research on Corporate Culture

A quick search on Google reveals that several hundred thousand articles have been written about corporate culture in recent years. The term "culture" has become so widely used it has lost some of its impact. According to the Small Business Encyclopedia, the technical definition of culture is "a set of values, beliefs, taboos, rituals and myths all companies develop over time" (2018). I prefer a much simpler definition. **Culture is how employees answer the question, "What's it like to work for that company?"** If enough employees answer this question in a similar fashion, you've got a pretty good feel for the health of an organization's culture.

Company and/or team cultures may be strict or lax, supportive or "cutthroat," and authoritarian or democratic. Unfortunately, according to the Gallup organization, as much as 70 percent of the American workforce is unhappy with their current culture (Gallup 2016). The majority of employees use words and phrases like "long hours, high stress, micromanagement and profit focused" to describe their current culture.

"When we have a Management Team meeting, we spend about 70 percent of our time focusing on culture and 30 percent on operations and the financials."

— Billy Salts, Owner,
Magic Valley Electric

Chapter 5 Diagnosing Team Culture

Business writer Seth Godin likes to say that there are basically two types of cultures: Front Row and Back Row. To understand his premise, think of a national sales team getting together for its annual meeting and the VP of Sales is about to kick things off. As various team members stroll into the auditorium, do they sit side by side in the front row or do they go to the back of the room and sit with two or three seats in between each other? Do they immediately begin chatting and laughing with one another or do they start working on their computers and/or phones? Once the meeting starts, is the VP lecturing and giving directives to the group or is there dialogue and debate throughout the session?

Does your team have a Front Row or Back Row culture?

Team vs. Organizational Culture

A common narrative I hear from leaders of specific departments is, "The organization as a whole is screwed up, but my team has a great culture." Is this possible? I suppose. However, usually when I start peeling back the layers, these supposed "high-functioning teams" aren't quite as terrific as the manager suggests. First of all, any manager who promotes his or her team, while publicly throwing the rest of the organization under the bus, isn't modeling effective leadership. Yes, other divisions of the company may be struggling, but huddling for a mutual admiration session with your own team is setting exactly the wrong example.

At Magic Valley Electric, throwing another team or individual under the bus is considered unacceptable. "We encourage people to express their opinions and even disagree with company strategy, as long as it is done constructively," said Salts. "However, what will kill morale and culture is allowing negative employees to gossip and criticize one another or the company behind the scenes."

Perhaps the strongest evidence that Magic Valley Electric's focus on culture is working is the low turnover rate among key employees and leaders. In the eight-year history of the company, very few leaders have left the organization. The turnover rate among employees is also extremely low in an industry where turnover is typically very high. "It's pretty simple," said Salts. "If you hire good people and create the right culture, people will want to stay and be a part of something special."

CHAPTER 6

Diagnosing Team Performance

"What gets measured gets done." – Peter Drucker

A common misperception in corporate America is that measuring the performance of different teams in a company will result in low morale within the organization. Additionally, the misunderstanding exists that comparing the performance of individuals within a given team will result in decreased employee morale. The assumption is that focusing too heavily on results will inevitably lead to dissension among employees. In fact, research has shown just the opposite. A study of teams in over 500 different organizations (National Institute of Ethics 2004) found that concentrating on measurable goals and holding teams and individual employees accountable resulted in a majority of employees within the organization experiencing higher morale.

In particular, high-achieving teams and their star employees perform their best work when performance is measured. Exceptional performers are driven to excel, and they tend to thrive when there is a tangible system for measuring success. According to the Harvard Business Review, top performers deliver about 400 percent more productivity than low to average employees. Logically, the last thing you want to do is create a culture where your highest performers are demotivated. As for your lowest-performing team members, they will certainly experience some discomfort in a results-oriented culture, and, frankly, that's exactly what you want.

Creating a Performance-Driven Culture

Healthy, productive teams have performance-driven cultures where goals are clearly defined. In a performance-driven culture, a majority of employees feel motivated and accountable and they strive to achieve. Meanwhile, low-performing team members either make improvements or eventually they move on. One of the reasons so many teams perform at substandard levels is that low performers are dragged along by their higher-performing colleagues. Creating a performance-driven culture will address this problem in a hurry.

The first challenge in creating a culture that focuses on results is defining the most important performance metrics to track. Common metrics include sales figures, error rates, and customer satisfaction scores. If you're a team leader and you aren't quite sure what you should be measuring, I would suggest you start by asking your boss how their success or failure is measured. In most cases, your team's metrics should align with those of your boss and his or hers should align with what senior management is measuring. Whatever metrics you select, it is vital that they are simple and understandable to the team as a whole, as well as its individual members.

"Your best employees tend to be competitive and they will perform at a high level if they know how they're being measured and what defines success."

— Dusty Standlee, President, Standlee Premium Western Forage

Chapter 6 Diagnosing Team Performance

Keep It Simple

At Standlee Premium Western Forage, one of the nation's largest producers of hay, they understand the "less is more" approach to metrics. According to Dusty Standlee, the company president, he learned a hard lesson when they tried to measure everything. "Years ago, we had two full-time IT guys that seemed to do nothing but create dashboards," Standlee said. "We were measuring thirty different things when, in reality, only a few were really important to our business."

Now the Standlee Company focuses almost entirely on two measurements. "Our key measurement on the Operations side is costs per ton. On the Sales side, we focus exclusively on what we call 'grow 15,' which means growing total sales by 15 percent a year." According to Standlee, by lasering in on these two key metrics, the employees have a clear understanding of the numbers that drive the business. "In the past, we had our employees confused as to what was really important to the company. Now, we talk about these two numbers in every meeting, and there's no uncertainty about what's important to our success."

Meaningful Rewards

The final, and perhaps most important, step in creating a performance-driven culture on your team is to establish a system of rewards. The more appealing the reward, the more likely team members will maintain motivation and meet or exceed performance standards. If your system of rewards is insufficient, employees may become indifferent.

At Standlee Premium Western Forage, incentives are paid twice a year. There's a simple formula and the bonuses are directly related to the goal of growing 15 percent annually. "We make sure that each salesperson owns their budget and forecast, and it meets or exceeds 15 percent growth," said Standlee.

As with the Standlee Sales Team, money is often the reward for high performance, and I certainly have no problem with that. However, team leaders should not always assume cash is king when it comes to incentivizing their workforce. Other reinforcers, such as praise, added responsibility, flexible schedules, and training opportunities may be equally motivating. In fact, a study conducted by the University of Chicago (Jeffrey 2009) found that noncash incentives in certain work environments can be as much as three times more motivating to employees.

However, regardless of how your organization chooses to reward employees, it is important that goals are simple and understandable. "Sometimes in the past, we've confused our employees with overly complicated business strategies," said Standlee. "In particular, your best employees tend to be competitive and they will perform at a high level if they know how they're being measured and what defines success."

CHAPTER 7

Top Ten Symptoms of a Sick Team

"Some teams get paralyzed by their need for complete agreement and their inability to move beyond debate."
– Patrick Lencioni, Author

I once did some consulting for a retail company that annually turned over more than 50 percent of its workforce. That's certainly a high number, even in an industry that routinely experiences turnover rates of 15 to 20 percent. However, when diagnosing the organization's turnover troubles, I quickly discovered something even more alarming than its annual turnover rate. It turns out that many of the 50 percent walking out the door were the organization's top performers, and to make matters worse, most of them were going to the competition.

Not all turnover is bad turnover. In fact, I like to see organizations weeding out about 10 percent of their low performers every year. However, if your company is hemorrhaging top performers, you are on the fast track to destruction. **There is no more obvious symptom that a team is unhealthy than a high turnover rate among top**

performers. High-performance turnover is number one on my list of the *Ten Symptoms of a Sick Team*. Below are ten of the signals that your team has some serious health issues:

1. Turnover among high performers
2. Excessive gossip
3. Minimal laughing and smiling
4. Finger pointing
5. Conflicting agendas
6. Weaponizing email
7. Micromanaging
8. Unresolved conflict
9. Imbalance in workload
10. Subgroups develop within team

Turnover Among High Performers: Top performers have plenty of options and the competition has their eyes on these people. If your team is chronically ill, your best people will find a healthier work environment.

Excessive Gossip: Every organization has gossip. However, if the rumor mill is the primary source of information in your workplace, you've got problems. Whispering in the break room and huddled meetings behind closed doors are signs of an unhealthy team.

Minimal Laughing and Smiling: Employees spend about a third of their lives working, so having a little fun is essential to team health. Research has also found that employees who regularly laugh at work are less stressed, more productive, and more creative (Kimmel and Associates 2015).

> *When I walk into meetings and the employees are quiet and the body language is poor, I get concerned. A quiet room usually means dysfunction.*

— Tabb Compton, COO, Scentsy

Chapter 7 Top Ten Symptoms of a Sick Team

Finger Pointing: On a healthy team, people can make mistakes and then take responsibility without being fearful. If deflecting responsibility is the norm, it's a warning sign that team members lack trust in one another and/or team leadership.

Conflicting Agendas: You can find out a lot about the health of a team by asking its members the question, "What are the three most important goals of your team right now?" If most of the group provides the same basic answer, the team is relatively well aligned. If the responses vary widely, your team members likely have competing agendas.

Weaponizing Email: Email is supposed to be a business communication tool, not a weapon for passive-aggressive communicators. If members of your team are criticizing colleagues and then copying half the office staff, your team is unhealthy.

Micromanaging: Trust is arguably the most important aspect of a team's culture, and you don't build trust by micromanaging. Micromanaging annoys employees and leads to burnout and eventually high turnover.

Unresolved Conflict: It's not unusual in corporate America to see conflicts fester for months or even years. Many of these conflicts could have potentially been resolved in a five-minute conversation. Healthy teams raise issues respectfully and resolve conflict in a timely manner. Unhealthy teams waste hundreds of hours every year due to unresolved issues.

Imbalance in Workload: If a handful of top performers are picking up the slack for their underperforming colleagues, your team is unhealthy. Your low performers will become lazier, and your top performers will eventually become resentful if the imbalance continues.

Subgroups Develop Within the Team: Certain team members will always gravitate toward one another because they have similar interests or complementary personalities. However, if cliques are developing, and certain members of your team are consistently being excluded, your team is unhealthy.

Tabb Compton, the Chief Operating Officer of Scentsy, one of the nation's leading multilevel marketing companies, has certainly seen many of the above symptoms over the course of his career. Compton is responsible for dozens of teams and more than 700 employees including warehousing, distribution, and quality. Before arriving at Scentsy, Compton leads numerous teams working as a senior executive for more than 25 years in health care, high tech, and retail.

So, with all this experience leading teams, what are the specific signs and symptoms Compton focuses on when assessing team health? "One of the first things I look at it is how leadership is behaving," said Compton. "When teams fail miserably, it's usually because executives don't want to take risks. They're too afraid to make decisions because they're worried about being vulnerable." According to Compton, the concern about taking risks often extends to the workforce as well. "When I walk into meetings and the employees are quiet and the body language is poor, I get concerned. A quiet room usually means dysfunction."

On the other end of the spectrum, Compton also gets suspicious when there's "a lot of chatter," but it's not constructive. "When people are constantly coming into my office talking about their colleagues, it's not a good sign. When this starts to happen, I confront it immediately. I get the employees together and tell them what I'm seeing. Most leaders don't want to create an uncomfortable moment to resolve a long-term problem."

Because Scentsy puts a premium on effective workplace communication and what Compton calls "the soft skills," morale among teams within the company has generally remained high. Turnover is significantly lower compared to many of their competitors and the company has won several "Best Places to Work" awards. "A healthy team is one where people are constantly bringing fresh ideas," said Compton. "When people feel their ideas are being heard, they get excited about being part of that team."

Section II

Assessing Team Health

CHAPTER 8

The Diagnosis: The Assessment of Team Health

"The strength of the team is each member.
The strength of each member is the team."
– Phil Jackson, Former NBA Coach

One often-overlooked reason for unhealthy teams is that organizations and their leaders lack insight into the current level of functioning of their work teams. It's virtually impossible to do team building without a measure of the current state of your team. With this in mind, I encourage you (and the other members of your team) to take the Assessment of Team Health (ATH). This tool consists of 30 questions and provides an overview of the current health of your team based on five components: 1) leadership, 2) communication, 3) trust, 4) culture, and 5) performance.

Assessment of Team Health

Use the scale below to score your team on the 30 items.

1. Strongly disagree
2. Disagree

3. Neither agree nor disagree
4. Agree
5. Strongly agree

Survey Items

1. Our team leader communicates clear goals and expectations.
2. Our team leader takes responsibility when things go wrong.
3. Our team leader runs productive meetings.
4. Our team leader is receptive to employee feedback.
5. Our team leader praises employees for good work.
6. Employee development is a priority for our team leader.
7. Team members engage in healthy debate.
8. Team members actively listen to one another.
9. Team members rarely engage in passive-aggressive communication (i.e., gossip, rumors, etc.).
10. Team members resolve conflict in a timely manner.
11. Team members utilize electronic communication appropriately (i.e., email, text messaging).
12. Team members actively share helpful information with each other.
13. Morale is high on our team.
14. Team members make sacrifices for the good of the team, rather than for personal gain.
15. Team members receive recognition from coworkers for good work.

> *If a wide variance exists between the highest and lowest subtest scores, this suggests a team has some significant areas of strength, but also weaknesses that need to be explored further.*

16. Team members rarely "kiss up" to the boss.
17. Members of our team rarely criticize other teams within the organization.
18. Members of our team have life balance.
19. Team members trust one another.
20. Team members share thoughts and opinions without fear of negative consequences.
21. Team members treat one another with respect.
22. Team members work collaboratively.
23. Team members are willing to apologize to one another.
24. Team members acknowledge personal weaknesses and are willing to ask for help.
25. Our team consistently meets or exceeds its goals.
26. Team members hold one another accountable for outcomes.
27. Team members are passionate about success.
28. Team members value performance metrics (i.e., sales goals, timelines, etc.)
29. Distribution of work on our team is relatively equal.
30. High performers are rewarded on our team.

Scoring Your Assessment

Once you have completed the ATH, add up your total number of points. The maximum possible score is 150 and the minimum possible score is 30.

30 to 60	61 to 119	120 to 150
Unhealthy	Stable	Healthy

Chapter 8 The Diagnosis: The Assessment of Team Health

Score Interpretation
(A Snapshot of Your Team's Health)

Unhealthy (30 to 60)   Your team needs immediate help! Morale is poor and team members are utilizing destructive forms of communication. Cliques exist and trust is low. Team goals and objectives are unclear, and the team leader is not holding low performers accountable. If your team is on the low end of "Unhealthy" (30 to 45), your condition is critical and you are bordering on total dysfunction.

Stable (61 to 119)   If your team is on the low end of "Stable" (61 to 80), you likely have some morale, leadership, and culture challenges that need attention. If you are in the midrange of "Stable" (81 to 100), your team is similar to most work teams in America. Morale is adequate and performance is solid, but unspectacular. If your team is at the high end of "Stable" (101 to 120), morale is generally high, the culture is relatively positive, and your team is likely performing at a high level.

Healthy (120 to 150) Assuming you were honest in assessing your team, congratulations! You're functioning in the top 10 percent of American work teams. Your team leader is outlining clear goals and objectives, communication is effective, morale is excellent, and your team is performing at a high level.

ATH (Subtest Scores)

Now that you have your overall score, which is a snapshot of how your team is functioning, it's time to dig into the details. Specifically, the next step is to examine your Team Health subtest scores. Remember, the Assessment of Team Health is made up of five different components: 1) leadership, 2) communication, 3) trust, 4) culture, and 5) performance. The maximum possible subtest score for any one component is 30 points. The minimum possible score is 6.

Leadership Subtest (Questions 1 to 6)

1.
2.
3.
4.
5.
6.
Total points:

Chapter 8 The Diagnosis: The Assessment of Team Health

Communication Subtest (Questions 7 to 12)

1.
2.
3.
4.
5.
6.
Total points:

Trust Subtest (Questions 13 to 18)

1.
2.
3.
4.
5.
6.
Total points:

Culture Subtest (Questions 19 to 24)

1.
2.
3.
4.
5.
6.
Total:

Chapter 8 The Diagnosis: The Assessment of Team Health

Performance Subtest (Questions 25 to 26)

1.
2.
3.
4.
5.
6.

Total points:

What Do Your Scores Really Mean?

While your overall ATH score provides a snapshot of team health, it is equally important to examine the subtest scores, as well as subtest variance, to truly understand how a team is functioning. For instance, a team might receive an overall score of 118, which is in the Stable Range, and just three points away from being considered Healthy. However, upon closer examination, you may discover a wide variance between subtests.

If a wide variance between the highest and lowest subtest scores exists, this suggests a team has some significant areas of strength, but also weaknesses that need to be explored further. It is crucial for team leaders to understand the nature of the weaker areas in order to improve overall team functioning.

Subtest Scores and Variance

It is not unusual for teams to report a wide variance between the Morale Subtest and the Performance Subtest. In Chapter 9, one of the case studies examines what I call a "Feel Good" Team, where employees report high morale, but their organization is not pleased with the team's level of performance. The reasons for the wide variance between morale and results on this team are explored in detail in the next chapter.

It is also common to see teams with significant variance between the Leadership Subtest and the Performance and Morale Subtests. Specifically, employees often rate their leader poorly, while simultaneously rating overall team performance and morale very high.

Finally, the Communication Subtest often ranks significantly lower than other subtests. In general, employees, even those who are relatively satisfied with their teams, believe communication can improve significantly. As a result, team members may rate areas like culture, performance, and trust high, while simultaneously ranking team communication very low.

Section III

Case Studies

CHAPTER 9

Case Study #1: The "Feel Good" Team

"The difference is conflict, an important yet overlooked aspect of all good communication." – David Meerman Scott, Author

The Executive Team of a large health care company scored a 124 on the ATH, which is solidly into the *Healthy* Range. The company was profitable and morale among employees was generally positive. So logically one might conclude that the Executive Team leading the organization was performing at a peak level. Well, not so fast.

While this team certainly had some significant strengths, including a Team Trust Subtest score of 28 and a Team Communication Subtest score of 27, the group had one very important Subtest that scored significantly lower than the rest. Specifically, the team scored just 18 on the Team Performance Subtest.

So, what accounted for the huge variance between the results score and the rest of the subtests? It turns out the various members of the Executive Team were warm, friendly, and caring people. Many of the team members were former clinicians, primarily nurses, and most said they had entered the health care field "to help people." While these are certainly admirable

Chapter 9 Case Study #1: The "Feel Good" Team

THE "FEEL GOOD" TEAM

OVERALL SCORE

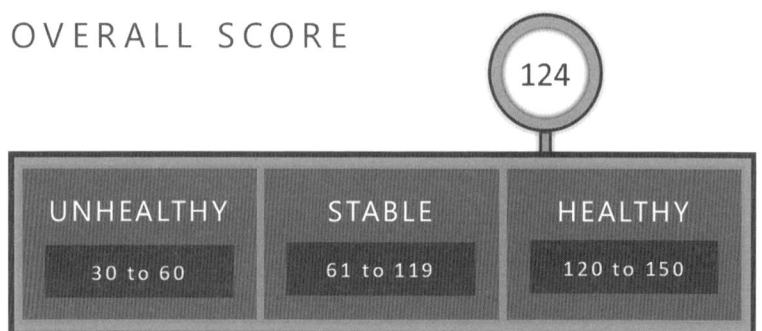

SUBTEST SCORE

- 18 PERFORMANCE
- 25 LEADERSHIP
- 26 CULTURE
- 27 COMMUNICATION
- 28 TRUST

> *The key to making team conflict a plus and not a minus is for group members to focus on substance rather than emotion.*

qualities to have in members of any executive team, the problem was that team members, including the CEO, were not holding one another accountable for achieving results.

Highest Ranked ATH Items

- Team members treat one another with respect.
- Team members work collaboratively.
- Morale is high on our team.
- Team members make sacrifices for the good of the team, rather than for personal gain.
- Team members receive recognition from coworkers for good work.

Lowest Ranked ATH Items

- Team members hold one another accountable for outcomes.
- Team members value performance metrics (i.e., sales goals, timelines, etc.)
- Distribution of work on our team is relatively equal.
- Team members engage in healthy debate.
- Team members resolve conflict in a timely manner.

"Nobody wanted to hurt anyone's feelings," said the CEO. "Collectively we were performing reasonably well, but we had individuals who weren't achieving results and those issues weren't getting addressed. Ultimately, it was on me. I was too worried about leading a feel-good team and not insisting on high performance."

When specific survey items were examined, we found that most team members answered strongly agree to items such as

"Team members work collaboratively" and "Team members treat one another with respect." Meanwhile, results were mixed when answering items such as "High performers are rewarded on our team" and "Team members hold one another accountable for outcomes." The net result was a team where members liked one another personally, but did not hold one another accountable for exceptional performance.

When we did a little more digging, we discovered that two of the seven Executive Team members, in particular, were not considered by their peers to be high performing. However, because the two were well-regarded and long-time contributors to the organization, difficult discussions related to performance were avoided.

Substantive Conflict vs. Emotional Conflict

Feel-good teams like the one described above are averse to conflict. They tend to view conflict as a bad thing and a threat to team morale. However, **multiple studies have found that conflict can be beneficial in improving team performance, as well as team unity.** The key to making team conflict a plus and not a minus is for group members to focus on substance rather than emotion.

Substantive conflict has to do with issues such as goals, tasks, and the allocation of team resources. For instance, a substantive conflict might occur when two team members disagree over how to best spend the department's budget. Conversely, emotional conflicts arise over things such as jealousy, insecurity, and annoyance. Two people who always seem to find themselves on different sides of issues because of personality differences is a common example of emotional conflict.

From a consulting standpoint, the recommendations for this team were obvious. Starting with the CEO, the team needed a lesson in assertive communication. Historically, team members had been passive about addressing low-performing colleagues. Instead of raising performance concerns, they simply tried to "pick up the slack" for coworkers who were missing goals and deadlines. In particular, the CEO had to be more direct with team members and engage in very specific performance discussions, especially with the two lower performers.

In addition, the team needed more clearly defined performance metrics. When I first asked the CEO about key metrics, she acknowledged that the team needed to set more specific, tangible goals. She said, "In the past, most of our metrics have been team goals, and some of them have been a little fuzzy." Like many organizations, this company may have had "fuzzy team goals" so that lower-performing individuals did not feel singled out. However, while team goals are certainly essential, so are individual metrics so that each member of the team is held accountable.

The CEO deserves credit. In spite of the fact that she was nonassertive by nature, she embraced the recommendations and began having difficult performance discussions and requiring more accountability. In addition to team goals, she set measurable goals for each manager of the executive team and some of the lower performers began to improve their performance. "Team chemistry and liking one another is obviously important," she said. "However, being a feel-good team can't come at the expense of performing at a peak level."

CHAPTER 10

Case Study #2: The "Passive-Aggressive" Team

"It's better to be alone than in bad company."
– George Washington

As far as workplaces go, this mid-sized technology company was an absolute snake pit. Unlike some nasty corporate environments, it wasn't so much that employees were intimidating or verbally abusive. In fact, it was pretty much the opposite. Instead, the company's Senior Executive Team had pretty much divided the organization into warring camps where groups of employees used rumor and gossip as their weapons of choice.

The Sales Department "despised" their coworkers in Operations. The IT employees thought their colleagues in Customer Service were "incompetent." Of course, few, if any, members of the Executive Team attempted to resolve the conflicts. Direct conversations were nonexistent. Instead, break room rants, closed-door whisper sessions, and biting email messages were the norm. In one case, we discovered that a rift had existed between two executives for more than a decade. Despite serving on the same leadership team, the two would not speak directly to one another, instead communicating through intermediaries.

Needless to say, the Executive Team of this organization did not score well on the ATH. The team's overall score was 53, which is well into the *Unhealthy* range. They scored just an eight on the Trust Subtest and nines on both the Communication and Culture Subtests. To put it bluntly, the team was a train wreck, a complete and total dumpster fire. In fact, calling this a "team" would have been overly generous. It was basically a set of individuals attempting to accomplish their own personal goals while simultaneously undercutting most of their peers.

An article by *Entrepreneur* magazine defines passive-aggressive communication as "a pattern of indirectly expressing negative feelings instead of openly addressing them" (T. Maylett 2017). **Common behaviors on passive-aggressive teams include sabotaging coworkers' efforts, procrastinating, and even delivering subpar work.** As the article correctly points out, unless handled directly, passive-aggressive behaviors rarely, if ever, resolve themselves.

> *The reality is that no organization will ever sustain a strong corporate culture if passive-aggressive communication is allowed to go unchecked.*

Chapter 10 Case Study #2: The "Passive-Aggressive" Team

THE "PASSIVE AGGRESSIVE" TEAM

OVERALL SCORE

SUBTEST SCORE

- (8) TRUST
- (9) CULTURE
- (9) COMMUNICATION
- (11) LEADERSHIP
- (16) PERFORMANCE

Chapter 10 Case Study #2: The "Passive-Aggressive" Team

Highest Ranked ATH Items

- Our team consistently meets or exceeds its goals.
- Team members are passionate about success.
- Team members value performance metrics (i.e., sales goals, timelines, etc.)
- Our team leader runs productive meetings.
- Employee development is a priority for our team leader.

Lowest Ranked ATH Items

- Team members work collaboratively.
- Team members trust one another.
- Team members share thoughts and opinions without fear of negative consequences.
- Team members treat one another with respect.
- Morale is high on our team.

So how did we possibly begin trying to turn around this passive-aggressive team that suffered from poor leadership, a complete lack of trust, destructive communication, and a toxic culture? Well, we started by conducting extensive interviews of all Executive Team members. In addition, we interviewed dozens of other employees within the organization who could provide insight into the dysfunction among the executives.

Predictably, what we found was that most of the senior executives were regularly the worst offenders when it came to engaging in passive-aggressive behavior. One common behavior was "bad-mouthing" their Executive Team peers in front of their individual business units. Another common occurrence was to write critical email messages about

Chapter 10 Case Study #2: The "Passive-Aggressive" Team

Executive Team colleagues and then copy half the company. Certainly not a unifying act.

Once we were able to identify the most common passive-aggressive behaviors, as well as the worst offenders, we called out the behavior. Then we trained the entire Executive Team in the art of effective communication. Specifically, the group needed to be taught how to deliver a direct, respectful message, whether communicating face to face, on the phone, or in an email. Once everyone had been formally trained, it became more difficult to "play dumb" and claim they didn't realize a certain mode of communication was destructive.

While we recommended that everyone be given a chance to improve their communication skills, with a team this dysfunctional, we weren't naïve enough to think everyone would embrace the process. One of our strongest recommendations was to terminate individuals who continued to display passive-aggressive behavior.

The reality is that no organization will ever sustain a strong corporate culture if passive-aggressive communication is allowed to go unchecked. I'll take a person who is a little bit aggressive any day of the week over someone who is gossiping, spreading rumors, and fueling chaos behind the scenes. In this instance, the company ultimately removed two of the Executive Team members who continued to behave destructively. Between the terminations, some additional training, and the hiring of some stronger leaders, the work environment has improved. However, passive-aggressive communication was the way that leaders and employees communicated for years, and those behaviors aren't unlearned overnight.

CHAPTER 11

Case Study #3: The "Frozen in Time" Team

"Never confuse movement with action."
— Ernest Hemingway

I was hard pressed not to fall asleep during the first management team meeting I attended at this mid-sized manufacturing company. Leader after leader provided a "department update," which basically consisted of events and tactics from the past week. Minimal discussion or debate. No focus on strategy. No innovation. Just a bunch of grind-it-out tacticians frozen in time. When the rare team member attempted to ask a question or make a strategic suggestion, he or she was immediately met with raised eyebrows and condescending looks. One gentleman basically encapsulated the entire two-hour meeting when he said, "We've done it this way for 20 years. Why would we do it any differently?"

After attending this initial meeting, it was clear why the company was losing business to its competitors. In addition to declining sales, the organization was also having challenges with recruiting and retaining employees, especially young, tech-savvy individuals. The company was

Chapter 11 Case Study #3: The "Frozen in Time" Team

basically stuck in time, attempting to do business the way it had for decades.

Organizations that are frozen in time typically display certain common characteristics, and this company demonstrated most of them, including:

- Fear: Team members who feel they are going to be mocked for suggesting a novel idea are highly unlikely to put forth that suggestion.
- Poor work environment: Stressed-out employees working long hours in bad working conditions will rarely demonstrate innovation. Employees in poor environments are focused on surviving the day, not building for the future.
- Insufficient communication: Employees will rarely support change if they don't understand the reasons for the change. Executive teams often institute major organizational change with an inadequate explanation as to why the change is occurring.
- Lack of connection: If team members like one another, they are more supportive, creative, and more willing to take risks. However, if members of the team don't like and support one another and feel little personal connection, risk taking is rare.

The Assessment of Team Health (ATH) scores with this team were predictable. The Trust Subtest was a ridiculously low seven. The Communication and Culture scores weren't much better, an eight and a nine, respectively. The overall ATH score was an *Unhealthy* 54. Basically, the organization had a toxic environment where new ideas weren't just discouraged; they were punished.

> *For frozen-in-time companies, any change is viewed as radical and usually faces serious resistance.*

Chapter 11 Case Study #3: The "Frozen in Time" Team

THE "FROZEN IN TIME" TEAM

OVERALL SCORE

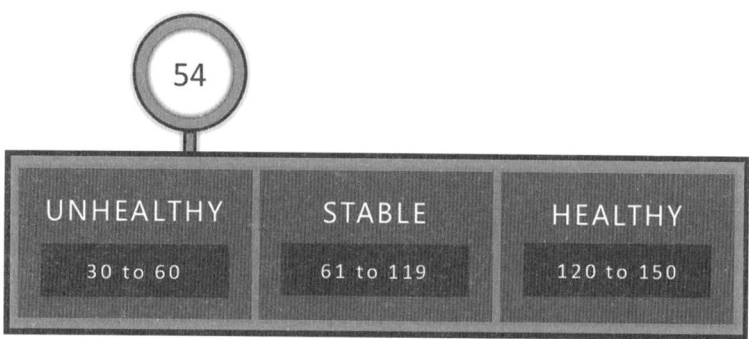

SUBTEST SCORE

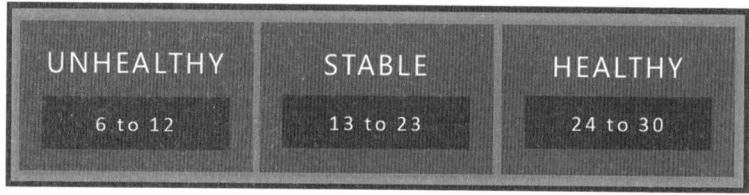

- (7) TRUST
- (8) COMMUNICATION
- (9) CULTURE
- (12) LEADERSHIP
- (18) PERFORMANCE

Chapter 11 Case Study #3: The "Frozen in Time" Team

Highest Ranked ATH items

- Team members hold one another accountable for outcomes.
- Team members are passionate about success.
- Team members value performance metrics (i.e., sales goals, timelines, etc.)
- Our team leader communicates clear goals and expectations.
- Our team leader takes responsibility when things go wrong.

Lowest Ranked ATH Items

- Team members share thoughts and opinions without fear of negative consequences.
- Team members acknowledge personal weaknesses and are willing to ask for help.
- Team members work collaboratively.
- Team members engage in healthy debate.
- Team members resolve conflict in a timely manner.

When we eventually interviewed company employees, we repeatedly heard comments suggesting that staff were avoiding risk taking at all costs. One gentleman said, "The key to succeeding around here is keeping your head down and not rocking the boat." Another woman said, "I just keep my opinions to myself and, as a result, I don't have any problems. That's why I've been able to keep my job." Employees had learned over the years that the key to survival was to follow the status quo.

Chapter 11 Case Study #3: The "Frozen in Time" Team

Obviously, a company with this type of environment lacks strong leadership. In this case, the owner was a third-generation family member. He was a nice enough gentleman in his early seventies, but he was very passive and, frankly, completely over his head. A couple of the long-time vice presidents were running the day-to-day operations of the organization, and they were determined to run things in a similar fashion to the past 20-plus years.

When we shared the ATH data with the owner, he wasn't particularly surprised. He knew the company culture had been growing worse and worse in recent years. However, he had no idea how to stop the slide. We made several recommendations, including the following:

- Infuse the organization with new blood: Specifically, we encouraged the hiring of leaders with experience in start-up and/or early stage companies. We also encouraged the hiring of outside speakers and consultants with a history of innovation.
- Change meeting formats: The weekly leadership meeting had become the symbol of everything that was wrong with the company. We encouraged the owner to scrap the meeting or institute one with a decidedly different feel and agenda.
- Reengage company ownership: The owner wasn't an effective leader, but he was a nice guy who was well-regarded by most employees. We advised him to become a more visible presence with employees and do "daily rounds," where he could speak to staff members out of the presence of some of the more toxic leaders.

Chapter 11 Case Study #3: The "Frozen in Time" Team

- Alter the system of compensation to encourage innovation: It's one thing for ownership to ask for employees to volunteer ideas; it's a whole different level when you compensate them for the ideas. In particular, a program was instituted that compensated employees whose manufacturing suggestions resulted in increased profits or decreased costs.

Our recommendations weren't earth-shattering. In fact, most of them were very obvious. However, for frozen-in-time companies, any change is viewed as radical and usually faces serious resistance. I wish I could say we convinced the owner to implement our suggestions and we helped improve the culture of the company. However, in the end, he decided against most of what we recommended. I think he genuinely wanted a better work environment for his employees. However, as is common with many "stuck" organizations, the fear of making significant change was simply too great. "I suppose we should probably make more of these changes," he said. "But we've been around for a long time so we must be doing something right."

Section IV

Transforming Your Team

CHAPTER 12

Do Activities and Exercises Build Teams?

"The ratio of We's to I's is the best indicator of the development of a team." – Lewis B. Ergen, Author

Organizations spend billions of dollars every year on team-building activities. Ropes courses, bowling matches, survival exercises, go-kart races, and escape rooms are just a few of the activities designed to help improve team functioning. The big question is "does team building work?" Unfortunately, that is difficult to answer because the research is mixed.

The American Psychological Association reports that "team building can help employees to feel valued and valued employees are more motivated and productive." In addition, results from the University of Central Florida and Army Research Institute study suggest that team building has "a positive moderate effect across all team outcomes."

Meanwhile, the Mars organization found that team-building events helped team members "feel closer for a brief period of time." However, the research found that "these bonds do not hold up under the day-to-day pressures of an organization focused on delivering results." Specifically, the research showed that vague goals related to team-building activities often failed to achieve the desired outcomes.

What Not to Do

While the data is mixed as it relates to the overall success of team-building activities, there are some definite dos and don'ts:

1) *Don't embarrass people.* Activities that participants feel are childish, like trust falls and sing-alongs, don't improve team morale or functioning; they just make most people feel foolish.

2) *Do customize the activity to fit the team's needs.* For instance, if the team is struggling to communicate effectively, select an activity that teaches participants better communication skills.

3) *Don't select a one-size-fits-all activity.* For example, if there are personal conflicts among members of the team, you may not want to select paintball as the activity, which will likely result in promoting competition rather than collaboration.

4) *Do activities regularly.* One grand team-building activity at the annual meeting does not make up for poor teamwork the rest of the year. Instead, engage in smaller team-building activities throughout the year.

5) *Don't try to resolve specific individual conflicts.* If two individuals on a team have conflict, a group session is not the place to resolve it. These conflicts should be resolved one-to-one, not in a group setting.

"Building a team is all about developing trust among the different members and that is something that develops over the course of time."

— Aaron Ricks, Operations Manager at Western Trailers

Chapter 12 Do Activities and Exercises Build Teams?

Aaron Ricks, Operations Manager at Western Trailers, is a leader who believes team building occurs over time instead of in one magical moment. "Team-building activities certainly have their place," said Ricks. "But building a team is all about developing trust among the different members and that is something that develops over the course of time."

Ricks has had plenty of experience building different work teams. He has eight direct reports and is responsible for 300 employees in a manufacturing environment at Western Trailers. Previously, Ricks worked several years in a global leadership role with John Deere, where he was accountable for leading teams made up of employees from around the globe. Building a cohesive team is hard enough in your own language and culture. Try doing so with a team made up of employees from different countries including India and Brazil.

"Whether you're leading a bunch of employees in Boise, Idaho, or an international group, I think the fundamentals are pretty much the same," said Ricks. "You've got to create an environment where people can express their opinions and take chances without fearing they're going to be ridiculed."

Ricks utilizes a variety of strategies to help create trust on his work teams, including 1) encouraging employees to know one another personally, 2) facilitating open communication, 3) establishing expectations for all team members, and 4) discouraging cliques. Ricks often puts team members together on "small projects" to begin the process of building trust and improving communication.

Chapter 12 Do Activities and Exercises Build Teams?

"On the best teams I've ever been a part of people felt free to express their ideas without being judged negatively," said Ricks. "That really isn't something that happens in a team-building exercise. It is something that develops over time and with a lot of hard work from the team leader as well as the members of the team."

CHAPTER 13

Turning Around a Troubled Team

"Getting good players is easy. Getting them to play together is the hard part." – Casey Stengel, Former Major League Baseball Manager

Nancy Koerner knows what it's like to take over a team with significant challenges. Koerner, Vice President of Health Services at Mary's Woods Senior Living, has been leading teams in the health care industry for more than 30 years. During that time, she has inherited a few teams that might make some managers rethink their desire to be in leadership. "I had a team earlier in my career that was really nasty," she said. "Some of the nurses were very resistant to change and were literally trying to sabotage what I was doing. It's hard to imagine that happening in a clinical setting, but it did."

According to Koerner, some of the specific behaviors that employees were engaging in included excessive gossip, sarcasm, and inappropriate use of email. Some nurses were even purposely failing to complete treatments in a timely manner in an effort to undermine department initiatives.

Chapter 13 Turning Around a Troubled Team

While Koerner certainly might have been justified in immediately disciplining or terminating members of her new team, she chose to wait. Instead, she sought to understand more about who and what was contributing to the negative culture. "I think a common mistake that leaders make is they make decisions about a team too quickly. In our culture we're in such a hurry to fix things. First it's important to understand the situation fully."

As part of her effort to better diagnose the team, Koerner began working side by side with the team members on a daily basis. She also engaged in a series of heart-to-heart discussions with the various team members. "I met with everyone in the department and laid out my expectations for being a member of the team," she said. "I also called attention to any destructive behaviors the various team members were participating in."

After the individual meetings, Koerner held a full-team session where team members were asked to "raise any unresolved issues" and get them out on the table. The session resulted in some "tears and intense discussion," but it began to improve team communication.

Koerner also spent the early days trying to identify "the influencers," both positive and negative. "If I was going to build a team, I needed to find out who the employees were listening to. I encouraged and supported the positive people and gave them additional responsibilities…And with the negative people, I had some very challenging conversations…Some of them aren't in the department any longer."

> *I think a common mistake that leaders make is they make decisions about a team too quickly. In our culture we're in such a hurry to fix things.*

— Nancy Koerner, Vice President of Health Services, Mary's Woods

Chapter 13 Turning Around a Troubled Team

Confront Destructive Communicators

As Koerner discovered, many low-performing teams are hotbeds of rumor, gossip, backbiting, and other forms of destructive communication. Aggressive communication (i.e., yelling, threatening, and giving ultimatums) has actually been on the decline in the past few decades in corporate America. However, passive-aggressive communication is alive and, in fact, thriving in the American workplace, and nothing will destroy your team faster than indirect, negative, behind-the-scenes communication.

The first steps in confronting passive-aggressive communication are defining the behavior and providing examples of the destructive forms of communication. Examples include 1) sarcasm, 2) negative nonverbal communication (i.e., eye rolling), 3) deliberate procrastination, 4) misuse of email (i.e., using the "copy" function to make colleagues look bad), and 5) withdrawing or quitting. Finally, passive-aggressive communicators need to be held accountable. Destructive behaviors should be addressed as they occur and employees need to be disciplined for their damaging communication behaviors. Teams rife with passive-aggressive communicators likely need extensive training on effective workplace communication to have any chance of becoming a team that communicates in a healthy manner.

Clarify Your Team's Purpose

In addition to communicating respectfully, teams need to understand their purpose. Many employees spend 40 or 50 hours a week on the job, yet despite the long hours, most employees know very little about the actual purpose of their work team. In fact, according to a study conducted by Franklin Covey, more than 55 percent of employees are unable to define the purpose of their team. If employees aren't certain why they're doing what they're doing, eventually concentration and motivation begin to dwindle, which ultimately impacts performance.

When employees don't understand the purpose of their team, the blame for this confusion can usually be traced to the organization's senior executives. Over the years, I've facilitated dozens of strategic planning sessions and they can be very helpful in defining high-level strategy. The problem is that the senior executives rarely communicate the strategic plan to the workforce. Typically, the strategic planning documents are filled with business school jargon and complex business strategies, which, candidly, are meaningless to most of the organization's employees. Instead, executives should do everything possible to simplify the organization's purpose and strategy and to communicate a handful of key company goals. Then, executives should utilize multiple mediums (town hall meetings, email, company newsletters, etc.) to communicate a simple company strategy. Managers and supervisors should be asked (or even required) to talk to their respective work teams about the purpose and goals of the company, and employees should also be given an opportunity to comment and provide input into company strategy.

Recognize and Reward

It's Psychology 101. If you want more of a certain behavior, positively reinforce it. Unfortunately, when members of a team have been performing poorly, they rarely receive praise

Chapter 13 Turning Around a Troubled Team

when they finally accomplish a task. Instead, the reaction from coworkers is generally more of an "it's about time."

However, this is a missed opportunity. In fact, the best chance you have of turning around a low-performing team or specific underperforming team members is to positively reinforce like crazy when performance improves. Specific strategies include 1) calling out individual/team achievements in company-wide email messages, 2) praising individuals privately in a specific and timely manner, and 3) catching low performers doing things right (not wrong). The last thing you may feel like doing is complimenting low performers. However, recognizing and rewarding improved performance likely provides your best opportunity to turn the behavior around.

Koerner has certainly utilized all of the above strategies over the years as she has worked to improve the health of certain teams. She emphasizes that it was rarely a single persuasive speech or an inspirational moment that improved the health of a team. Instead, it was more of a long, slow grind. "I wish there were some magical words to make a team's problems go away, but there's not. Instead, I spend time getting to know the employees, understanding what motivates them, and working alongside them. Usually, it's just hard work."

CHAPTER 14

Transitioning from Average to Elite

"There is immense power when a group of people with similar interests gets together to work toward the same goals."
– Idowu Koyenikan, Author

We know a lot of interesting facts about teams. For instance, research has demonstrated that the ideal team size is between four and nine people. Studies have also found that that mixed age teams are generally more successful than teams with just younger participants. We also know that teams tend to be more productive when they are in close physical proximity as opposed to working remotely. Thousands of studies have been conducted on teams and teamwork, yet a huge percentage of work teams remain unhealthy. However, **despite the ongoing struggle to form healthy, highly functional teams, corporate America continues its quest to find the recipe for forming and maintaining elite teams.**

Talent vs. Team

Let's not kid ourselves. The Chicago Bulls wouldn't have won multiple NBA Championships without Michael Jordan. The Rolling Stones wouldn't be one of the greatest rock bands of

Chapter 14   Transitioning from Average to Elite

all time without Mick Jagger. Talent matters. On all truly elite teams, there are exceptionally talented individual members. However, athletics, entertainment, and the business world are all littered with groups of highly talented individuals who weren't able to come together to form an exceptional team.

So how do you transform a team that is reasonably healthy and is functioning at an average level, to one that is elite? Assuming for a moment that the team consists of sufficiently talented individuals, then it is crucial that the team develops trust and a culture that supports certain behaviors and characteristics. The Gallup organization has been studying elite teams extensively for decades, and they have found that exceptional teams almost always have the following traits:

1) Engage in healthy debate: The most successful teams disagree. Sometimes they disagree often and passionately, and that is a good thing. According to Gallup, what differentiates elite teams from dysfunctional ones is that the team doesn't fragment when members disagree. Instead, they gain strength from the debate.

2) Keep the larger goal in mind: Gallup found that members of elite teams tend to have widely varying opinions, but they have something in common. They are able to put their personal agendas and egos aside and focus on what is in the best interest of their organization.

3) Offer opportunities for development: Exceptionally talented people always want to be improving. They are intellectually curious and motivated by new challenges. According to Gallup, teams are at risk for talented members becoming disengaged or even leaving if they feel they aren't developing.

"The most successful teams disagree. Sometimes they disagree often and passionately, and that is a good thing."

Chapter 14 Transitioning from Average to Elite

4) Have lives outside of work: Gallup discovered that members of elite teams work extremely hard, but they also consider their lives balanced. Specifically, they bring the same level of energy to their family and personal lives as they do to their work lives.

5) Embrace diversity: Gallup found that teams with diverse educational and cultural backgrounds were more likely to achieve elite status. While gender and race differences are important, it is equally important for elite teams to be made up of individuals with different leadership, communication, and problem-solving styles.

6) Attract more talent: Want to find an elite team? According to Gallup, look for the team that everyone wants to be on. Because elite teams have high-energy, successful cultures, they tend to be a magnet for other talented employees.

Many teams have the capability to be elite. However, they remain mediocre because they fail to create an environment where the above behaviors are commonplace. "People are dying to work on great teams," said Jack Welch, the legendary CEO of GE. "They want to be part of an engaged and successful team. They want to have fun, learn, grow and be rewarded for their contributions. The only question is, will they find that in your team or will they have to look elsewhere?"

Welch, who grew GE revenues by more than 4,000 percent during his time running the company, largely agreed with the Gallup research when it comes to building elite teams. He too believed in the importance of concepts such as "knowing the larger goal or game plan" and direct debate and communication "to let people know where they stand on the team." However,

Chapter 14   Transitioning from Average to Elite

Welch believed elite teams have one additional characteristic in common: they celebrate.

"Most teams don't understand the tight link between celebrating small successes along the way and achieving the big one at the end," said Welch. "Celebrations teach team members what it feels like to win, which is, well, a very good feeling. It makes people want to win more. In fact, they never want the feeling to go away. So they do everything to keep winning."

Conclusion

"A moment's insight is sometimes worth a life's experience."
– Oliver Wendell Holmes Sr.

I started this book with a story about Traci McGregor, a nurse leader who was caught in the middle of the COVID-19 crisis. McGregor and her leadership team performed admirably, testing and treating hundreds of patients under frightening and stressful circumstances. "They all stepped up," said McGregor. "A couple of my team members basically refused to go home, and all of them showed tremendous courage."

The story of McGregor and her team was inspiring, but we also know it is rare. Research tells us that only about 10 percent of teams perform at a truly elite level while more than 60 percent are largely dysfunctional. Meanwhile, approximately 30 percent of teams perform at an average level.

In spite of these less than impressive statistics, corporate America's emphasis on teams isn't going away. According to research conducted by the *Harvard Business Review* (Hass and Mortensen 2016), the bulk of modern work is conducted by teams. "One study states that "collaborative activities have ballooned by 50 percent or more over the last two decades and that, at many companies, more than three quarters of an employee's day is spent communicating with other colleagues."

The bottom line is that the business world's quest to build healthy, successful teams is not slowing down. In fact, it is accelerating. As to why so many teams are unhealthy, the reasons are numerous. The most common challenges include poor leadership, destructive forms of communication, finger pointing, and competing agendas. Some teams continue to be sick for years or even decades because conflict goes unresolved.

The good news is that almost all teams have the capability to become healthier. Several of the leaders I interviewed for this book talked about their ongoing battle to improve team health. Dusty Standlee, President of Standlee Premium Western Forage, said, "Hell, our management team has done more wrong than right over the years. But we learn from our mistakes and we try to do better the next time." Billy Salts, President of Magic Valley Electric said, "If you want to create a great management team or a great company culture, you can't get satisfied. We're always trying to evaluate how we're doing and make improvements."

What these leaders understand is that the key to improving the health of your team is to gain information. A leadership team can't simply set out to improve teamwork for the sake of improvement alone. Instead, the team leader and its members must first know which components they are trying to improve. Does the team lack trust? Do team members need to communicate more effectively? Is your team failing to achieve results?

If you decided to read this book, you may be on a team that is unhealthy or just barely stable. You might even be leading such a team. The Assessment of Team

> *The good news is that almost all teams have the capability to become healthier.*

Health can provide a snapshot into your team's current level of functioning. Encourage your team members to complete the survey and begin taking a detailed look at how your team is functioning when it comes to the five key components: 1) leadership, 2) communication, 3) trust, 4) culture, and 5) performance. Gather and analyze your data and carefully examine your team strengths and weaknesses. Don't be content being a member of an unhealthy team. It's time to diagnose your team and begin implementing the strategies outlined in this book. It's time to begin transforming your team.

Sources

1. Solomon, Lou. 2016. "Two-thirds of Managers are Uncomfortable Communicating with Employees." *Harvard Business Review*, March, 2016.
2. Schwantes, M. 2016. "Why People Quit Their Jobs." *Inc Magazine*, December, 2016.
3. Parisi-Carew, E. 2009. *The One Minute Manager Builds High Performing Teams.*
4. Pencak, Silvia. 2017. "Top Ten Signs of Poor Leadership." (Blog Post).
5. Godin, Seth. 2016. "The Front Row Culture." (Blog Post, March, 2016).
6. Whitney, John, O. 2017. "The Leadership Factor of Turnarounds." (Blog Post, October, 2017).
7. Rath, T. & Conchie, B. 2009. "What Strong Teams Have in Common." Gallup Study, March, 2009.
8. Valdes-Dapena, C. 2018. "Stop Wasting Your Money on Team Building." *Harvard Business Review*, September, 2018.
9. Welch, J. 2016. "How to Make Your Team THE Place to Be." (Article, October, 2016) *Jack Welch Learning Institute.*

Sources

10. Welch, J. & S. Welch, S. 2020. "How to Build a Winning Team." *Newsweek*, 2020.
11. Olson, L. 2012. "Do Corporate Team Building Events Really Work?" *Newsweek*, June, 2012.
12. Deborah D., Cameron K., Eduardo S., Huy, L., Burke, R., & Goodwin, G. 2016. University of Central Florida and Army Research Institute Study.
13. Plummer, M. 2018. How are You Protecting Your High Performers from Burnout? *Harvard Business Review*, June, 2018.
14. Reina, D. & Reina, A. 2017. "Why Trust is Critical to Team Success." *Center for Creative Leadership* Report, May, 2017.
15. Bryant, A. 2018. "How to Build a Successful Team." *New York Times*, September, 2018.
16. Maylett, T. 2017. "Eight Solutions for Managing a Passive-Aggressive Team." *Entrepreneur*, November, 2017.
17. Cross, R., Rebele, R. & Grant, A. 2016. "Collaborative Overload." *Harvard Business Review* February, 2016.

Recognition of Interviewees

- Special thanks to the great leaders who shared their time, knowledge, and experiences so that I could write this book.

Tabb Compton, COO .... Scentsy

Mary Chronin, Associate .... St. Luke's Health System Vice President of Operations

Nancy Koerner, Vice President .... Mary's Woods of Health Services

Nancy Lebold, Vice President .... Food 4 Less of Merchandising

Traci McGregor, RN, Emergency .... St. Luke's Hospital Department Director

Teresa Mitzel, Head of .... Syngenta Seeds Biological Operations

Aaron Ricks, Operations Manager .... Western Trailers

Billy Salts, President .... Magic Valley Electric

Dusty Standlee, ... Standlee Premium Western Forage President